Destroying Progressivism:
A Strategy

Destroying Progressivism: A Strategy

By

Jefferson White

Cover Design by Jefferson White
Photo: "Into the Jaws." Franklin D. Roosevelt Library
Public Domain Photographs, 1882 - 1962

ISBN-13: 978-1726291217
ISBN-10: 1726291219

1. Politics   2. Computer Technology and Politics
3. Progressivism

Table of Contents

Grand Strategy - 11

Progressivism is not primarily a system of belief. It is a power strategy based upon turning over all social and political power to a central authority. Thus to radically decentralize society is to destroy progressivism. And the possibility that American society can be radically decentralized is very real. It only requires taking the next step in the technological revolution.

The Strategic Situation - 16

Progressives now control all the major institutions of American life. Therefore the replacement of those institutions has become imperative. But there is currently only one real strategic contest underway: the battle for control of who reports the news. The old, progressive mass media are dying and the progressive Big Tech platforms are attempting to take their place. The anti-progressive online media are locked in mortal combat with Big Tech.

Immediate Strategies - 35

There are steps that can be taken by anti-progressives today to break the power of Big Tech. Here is a short outline of some of those steps.

Urbit: Creating A New Internet - 48

One answer to a centralizing Internet is to create a new and radically decentralized Internet to replace it. Although such a project is neither easy nor simple, it is surprisingly easier and simpler than one might imagine. Welcome to Urbit.

Smart Contracts: Merging Agreement and Execution - 59

One way to destroy a bureaucratic political and social order, in which all contractual relationships involve third party interventions, is to completely eliminate third party interventions. Welcome to the smart contract revolution.

The Blockchain: Establishing Relationships Without Trust - 68

Blockchains are unalterable by design. Thus any smart contract placed on a blockchain cannot be altered. Nor can that smart contract execute except according to unalterable rules that are permanently embedded in that blockchain. Welcome to the blockchain revolution.

Cryptocurrencies: Decentralizing Money - 79

A cryptocurrency is digital money embedded on a blockchain. Therefore it cannot be counterfeited, inflated, or controlled by any third parties, including governments. Security of ownership is guaranteed. Welcome to the cryptocurrency revolution.

Ethereum: Creating the Decentralized Society - 85

The goal of the Ethereum blockchain is to create a radically decentralized society made up of millions of smart contracts. Ethereum thus allows the creation of a new kind of organization: the DAO or Decentralized Autonomous Organization. Welcome to Ethereum.

Hashgraph: Beyond the Blockchain - 94

Is hashgraph the revolutionary next step beyond the blockchain?

Summary and Conclusion - 105

A summary and overview of the coming revolution.

Grand Strategy

The Grand strategy defines the goal or purpose of a war. All other strategies exist in support of the grand strategy.

The grand strategic goal in the war against progressivism is the destruction of the progressive control of American society.

Today's American progressives are preparing for their final consolidation of power. It does not matter that Donald Trump is president or that the Republicans control both houses of Congress, as well as most state legislatures. Progressives consider this to be only a temporary interruption of that final consolidation, which will be based upon their control of the media, education, and the government bureaucracy. They are also counting on their ability to introduce tens of millions of illegal aliens more into the United States who will then vote for the permanent expansion of progressive control over society. When progressives next take the presidency, they intend to use that office to ensure, through the deliberate and permanent suppression of anti-progressive opposition, the creation of their final revolution.

After 1932, the process of consolidating all political and social authority in the national state became an ongoing progressive project for the next eighty years. But it remained an incremental project for decades, because there were too many constitutional and social roadblocks standing between progressives and any final consolidation of power.

Those roadblocks are now largely dissolved. More importantly, progressives are mentally primed for a final victory as the political end game comes into view. From this point forward, progressives intend to no longer tolerate any public statements of belief, or any public actions, which directly contradict progressive beliefs. Even today, although out of power in Washington D.C., progressives are busy perfecting social methods of public intimidation and public violence. When another progressive president is elected, the full weight of the national state, and of that state's deputized social authorities, will be used to suppress that dissent.

As the end game approaches, the beliefs of progressives are becoming more and more surreal, even as society becomes more and more dysfunctional. Although the formal end game of the progressives is to create the final progressive revolution, the real end game will be the creation of a permanent anarcho-tyranny. This is a society that will be at once lawless and excessively governed by law. Under anarcho-tyranny, it will be the law-abiding who will be punished by the state, while the lawless will be under state subsidy.

Which raises the following grand strategic question: How are we to create a revolution that will destroy the progressive control of American society?

In the nineties, it was believed by many of those who best understood the new technological revolution that the computer and the Internet would destroy the centralized business corporation and the centralized state. The individual as such would now be able to deal online directly with other individuals without the need for intermediate institutions. The power of the giant corporations and of the central state would decline as this radical disintermediation of society occurred.

But things did not turn out that way, at least in the short run.

Instead, over the past two decades, a small number of mega-corporations have arisen online to become the intermediaries through which people interact. These new mega-corporations are not only hyper-centralized in their organization, but also employ the technologies of mass data collection and continual online surveillance to track everything that everyone does online. At the pinnacle of this system are the security agencies of the national state, which also track and record every individual online.

Thus the most immediate result of the technological revolution has been the hyper-centralization of social and political power.

However, this is not the complete story. For there are also tens of millions of people online who are organizing and communicating outside of those corporate platforms, and also within them, in ways never before possible. A radical decentralization of power and authority is also going on.

Take the news media as an example. During most of the twentieth century, the progressive-controlled major newspapers, major newsmagazines, broadcast networks, and major wire services were the institutions that decided not only what the news of the day would be, but how that news would be interpreted. This progressive system is now in radical decline. Today, there are tens of thousands of anti-progressive news sources online that continually contradict the progressive news narrative. Roughly one third to one half of the American people now routinely ignore the news of the major media and receive much or most of their news from these alternative news sources. Trump's election became possible only because nearly half the American people agreed with him that the major media were nothing more than "fake news."

This is also why, in the wake of Trump's election, that the progressive corporations which control the major online platforms are now actively engaged in strategies to suppress the anti-progressive media online. These corporations are involved in a major effort to suppress, to downgrade, or even to remove, those online news sources that contradict the progressive narrative.

And yet, those who are the most familiar with the ongoing technological revolution continue to believe that a radical decentralization of power is coming. They argue that innovations in software are only now beginning to subvert, and that they will ultimately destroy, the Big Tech platforms.

Are they right in this belief?

It does seem that, if the progressives' control of American society is to be destroyed, it will be through the use of this new technology.

In the final analysis, the progressive control of American society is inseparable from their ability to centralize political and social power. Progressives themselves fully believe that all such authority must be centralized in order for them to create their final revolution. Progressivism ultimately stands or falls, not on the persuasiveness of its system of beliefs, which are increasingly nonsensical, but on their ability to centralize power.

Thus the coming destruction of the progressive control of American society and the coming technological decentralization of that society are the same revolution.

The Strategic Situation

All American institutions of consequence are now under progressive control, except for America's political institutions.

All publicly acceptable discourse is now governed by progressive assumptions, assumptions that are no longer permitted to be publicly questioned. The so-called "conservative" in today's America is now primarily concerned with maneuvering within the limits of this permitted discourse. And the limits are narrowing to a vanishing point.

Currently, the only successful anti-progressive strategy is to be found in the rise of the anti-progressive media online. Of course, there is the temporary Trump presidency and the Republican control of Congress. But progressives control everything else of consequence in American society. And when they once again control the presidency, their final consolidation of power will begin.

That is the strategic situation.

Progressives fully believe that they have won the "culture wars." They fully believe that they are in the process of rolling up whatever remains of a genuine opposition to their control of American society. Progressives fully believe that in the future there will be no genuine opposition to their control, since they intend to suppress that opposition. And they are not wrong to believe these things.

Progressive confidence is energized by a spineless Republican Party, now largely controlled by a semi-progressive corporate class. The Republican Party has become largely a pseudo-opposition. The majority of elected Republicans effectively belong to a Uniparty that controls all the elected branches of government, except for the Trump presidency.

Intellectual conservatism, a movement founded sixty years ago to oppose progressivism, now largely acts to conserve the progressive revolution of 1932-2008. Most intellectual conservatives have become the right wing of the progressive revolution.

Conservatives argue for the principles of limited government, while acting to conserve a regime of unlimited government. Conservatives argue for judicial restraint, while acting to conserve a regime of un-limited judicial authority. Conservatives argue for sexual restraint, while acting to conserve a culture of unlimited sexualization. Conservatives argue for the primacy of individual freedom, while acting to con-serve a culture in which individual identity is now a social construction of the state.

Is it any wonder that the post-conservative right calls conservatives "cuckservatives?"

Any genuine opposition to the progressive control of American society begins with the recognition that this control must be destroyed. It is this revolutionary understanding that the cuckservative rejects.

During the years of the Obama presidency, the national administrative state was finally placed beyond effective democratic control. But this event had been in the cards since 1932. All historical change is generational and we are now four generations past the New Deal. The absence of constitutional government since that era is now the effective political experience of the American people. The Obama administration merely marks the final transition to an administrative dictatorship. It no longer really matters who is president, although Trump is temporarily raising havoc with progressive control of the administrative state.

During the Obama era, congressional Republicans did not lift a finger to oppose the final transition of power to the administrative state. During the Obama era, most congressional Republicans, and all congressional Democrats, effectively ceased to be the representatives of the people and became the representatives of the administrative state to the people.

We are now well into the Trump presidency. And it is clear that progressives continue to control most of the administrative state. Even where Trump has success-fully taken control of parts of the administrative state, his control is ephemeral. Once Trump is gone, the final progressive revolution begins.

The Trump presidency is an interregnum.

The Trump presidency is a breathing space that is allowing anti-progressives to prepare for the coming storm. But the Trump presidency is also a decisive shock to the progressive system, since it demonstrates that American politics is not completely under their control. But there are no other politicians waiting in the wings who personify Trump's visceral rejection of progressivism. Once Trump is gone, the democratic revolt against progressivism will be over.

Current Anti-Progressive Strategy

Once again: The only current battle of consequence being fought by anti-progressives is being waged by the online anti-progressive media.

And although the anti-progressive media have been able to directly challenge progressive control of the news, they are far from being able to destroy that control. A majority of the American people continue to get much or most of their news from the progressive media. The current strategy of the anti-progressive media has been to consolidate their gains while trying to find ways to extend their reach to a greater share of the population. But this has become a war of attrition.

The current strategy of those progressives who control the major online platforms is to deny anti-progressives access to those platforms. This strategy, which is in the process of ramping up, is threatening to drive the anti-progressive media from the field.

Had Hillary Clinton become president, the current battle for control of the news would be a far worse. Under Clinton, the full weight of the administrative state, and of her newly appointed progressive judges, would have been joined to the power of Big Tech in a decisive campaign to rid the Internet of the anti-progressive media. As it is, even with Trump as president, Big Tech has doubled down in its efforts to throttle anti-progressives online. But since Trump is president, Big Tech is forced to pursue this strategy without governmental support.

The current battle for control of the news is being fought on two levels.

First, the anti-progressive online media have been remarkably successful in publicly discrediting the progressive media narrative. Anti-progressive news now reaches one third to one half of the American people on a continuous basis and often influences the middle third of the electorate. At this level of battle, the anti-progressive media have gone from strength to strength. Trump's election alone demonstrates that at least half of the American people no longer pay any attention to the major media, because if they did Trump would not be president.

Second, the anti-progressive online media are now attempting to extend their reach to a solid majority of the American people. But this has been a far less successful enterprise. Little of consequence has been accomplished toward this goal, while the goal recedes as Big Tech acts to suppress the anti-progressive media on its platforms and beyond.

Working together, the old major media and the Big Tech corporations have major advantages in this fight.

First, the old major media have retained their authority to decide what "the news of the day" will be and how that news will be interpreted, or at least they retain that authority in progressive circles and in cucked Republican circles. The main progressive gatekeepers of the old media are: ABC, CBS, NBC, NPR, CNN, the *New York Times*, the *Washington Post*, the Associated Press, and Reuters. By calling these corporations gatekeepers, we mean that they are the organizations that decide what the "news of the day" will be and what the "proper interpretation" of that news will be.

To this list we should also add the Big Tech gatekeepers: Facebook (which owns Instagram, WhatsApp, and Messenger), Google (which owns YouTube and Android), Twitter, Microsoft (which owns Bing), and Apple (which owns iPhone).

By the year 1950, progressive control of the American news media was firmly in place. In that year, a relative handful of radio and (emerging) television networks, together with the major wire services, the major newspapers, and the major newsmagazines, possessed an effective monopoly on the news. In part, this was the result of the decline of local and regional newspapers, which had once dominated the dissemination of news. Local papers now relied on news that was written by the major wire services and news syndicates. However, in large part, the progressive control of the news was the result of the rise of the major broadcast networks, and in particular of the big three television networks, which became the centralized locus for defining the news of the day.

This rise of the networks was the direct result of administrative state regulations, which were written to ensure that there would be just a handful of networks. These regulations also required that the broadcast networks be "politically neutral." What this actually meant was that a soft-progressive version of the news became the American news standard, a system of controlled news that would dominate the second half of the twentieth century. Progressive broadcast news, fed by other progressive media, became the news for most Americans.

In the late eighties, the Reagan administration repealed the edicts that mandated "political neutrality" in broadcasting. The anti-progressive news breakout thus began with Rush Limbaugh, who became the first national anti-progressive alternative to the major news media. Twenty million Americans were soon listening to his daily three hour news commentaries. Other anti-progressive radio talk shows soon followed and grew major audiences. But progressive talk radio failed to find a major audience, since most progressives already got their news from the major media.

During the nineties, Fox News became the first center-right television cable news network. Progressives, then and now, describe Fox News as a "far right" news service. But as UCLA Political Science Professor Tim Groseclose showed, in his ground-breaking social scientific study, *Left Turn: How Liberal Media Bias Distorts the American Mind* (2011), Fox News (the news show itself and not the political commentators) stood at about the 40th percentile of political bias on a right to left axis. In short, although 60% of the American people were to the left of Fox News, 40% of Americans were to the right of Fox News.

Every other major news organization in Groseclose's study (NBC, CBS, ABC, NPR, CNN, the *New York Times*, and the *Washington Post*) ran the gamut from the 60th percentile to the 85th percentile in progressive news bias. In other words, from sixty to eighty-five percent of the American people were to the right of the major news media.

During the first decade of the new century, the Internet became a major player in the dissemination of news. Tens of thousands of blogs, Twitter accounts, and online videos appeared, created by progressives and anti-progressives alike. But this new medium favored anti-progressives simply because progressives already controlled the old media. And because the balance of media power was now shifting online, and was splintering into myriads of sources, thousands of anti progressives were finding their public voices for the first time. Anti-progressive auteurs of all kinds were creating huge online followings.

Simultaneously, the nature of the progressive media was changing. This was because online progressives were now free from the political constraints imposed upon the old major media. They no longer had to pretend to be "neutral interpreters" of the news.

Indeed, online progressives now considered it offensive to believe that the proper interpretation of the news could be anything other than a progressive interpretation. The old, fake "political neutrality" of the major media was no longer viable.

The old major media were also discovering this heady new freedom. But they were claiming that "neutral reporting" and progressive reporting were the same thing. And since moderate and conservative Americans were already leaving the old major media in droves, it no longer made sense to pretend to be anything other than progressive. And that, in turn, only accelerated the departure of non-progressive Americans from the major media, which allowed them to become even more explicitly progressive.

The 2016 presidential election was the turning point in the media wars. Under the pressures of that campaign, the old major media became complete shills for Hillary Clinton. This would have appalled the progressives of the older era, who greatly valued the appearance of media neutrality. This also meant that, for that half of the American people who voted for Donald Trump, the major media were now universally regarded, in Trump's famous words, as being "Fake News."

Current Limitations of the Anti-Progressive Media

However, despite the collapse of the old major media, progressives still retain overall control of the news narrative.

There are four reasons for this.

First, the old major media, despite a radical decline in market share, continue to attract tens of millions of viewers and readers. They are still the elephant in the room in terms of sheer audience size.

Second, the old major media are still the progressive news command center, despite the rise of an online progressive media. Online progressives now provide much of the news that feeds the old major media, which then repackages their stories and tones them down for popular consumption. At the same time, however, the old major media continue to act as a clearing-house for defining the news of the day for the overall progressive media. It is this partnership between the old major media and the new online progressive media that continues to define the continuing progressive control of the news for nearly half of the population.

Third, the online anti-progressive media are decisively handicapped in that they mostly consist of small organizations and individuals. They are also largely self-funded, whether relying on donations or by running online ads. The progressive media, online and off, enjoy a far greater access to the big advertising dollars and to the millions of dollars that are available from rich progressive donors and foundations. For example, Amazon billionaire Jeff Bezos has personally spent tens of millions of dollars to keep the Washington Post afloat. That expenditure not only allows him to own one of the major newspapers that gets to define the news, but which is also the newspaper of the Washington, D.C. power brokers. The Mexican billionaire, Carlos Slim, plays a similar role with regard to the New York Times.

And yet, the online balance of media power has shifted against progressives.

Because the anti-progressive media now continuously reach one third to one half of the American people, the number of consciously anti-progressive Americans is rapidly growing. During the second half of the twentieth century, in an era in which progressives controlled the news, most non-progressive Americans were only latently anti-progressive. They may have grumbled about news bias and voted for Reagan, but they expected liberals to define the news. But the one third to one half of the American people who now follow the anti-progressive online media are in the process of becoming radicalized. Trump's election is a sign of that radicalization.

Fourth, and this is the most decisive strategic advantage of the progressive media, Big Tech is now fully engaged in removing as much of the anti-progressive media from their public platforms as possible, as well as in removing them from the Internet as far as that is possible. Big Tech is now working in over-drive to achieve this strategic goal. And since most Internet traffic flows through the Big Tech platforms, and since Big Tech controls how websites are stored and made available online, this counterattack is a major strategic blow against the anti-progressive media.

The only real question is whether Big Tech has the means and the will to accomplish this strategic goal. There is also the question of how the anti-progressive media will act in response to this strategy.

The Internet began as an experiment in decentralized, peer-to-peer networking. During the early nineties, individual computers directly connected to other individual computers without the need for any intermediary. This first Internet was a system of radically decentralized communications. However, with the rise of mass public use of the Internet, peer-to-peer communications began to recede as Americans began to join the huge, controlled platforms created by Big Tech. These platforms have become the Internet for the majority of Americans.

Facebook alone has over two billion people on its platform. And the progressives who control that platform are attempting to deal with the stark reality that tens of millions of anti-progressives use their platform to share anti-progressive news and information. Google and Bing, the two major online search engines, are now employing algorithms to downgrade search results that do not fit the progressive narrative. Twitter has become the most overt online censor of anti-progressive users, through a continuing campaign to ensure that anti-progressive "tweets" cannot be found, through a process that is called "shadow-banning." Twitter is also engaged in the banning of even prominent anti-progressives from its platform. Google-owned YouTube is involved in a major effort to demonetize anti-progressive videographers, removing their ability to make a living by running ads. YouTube is also engaged in degrading the ability of viewers to find anti-progressive videos on their site, and is also engaged in the outright banning of anti-progressive videos.

Before the 2016 election, much of this progressive censorship already existed, but was unsystematic. In part, this was because Big Tech progressives were still committed to a vision of creating an Internet based upon freedom of speech. And since this commitment was not entirely hypocritical, they found themselves on the horns of a dilemma. While wanting to be celebrated as avatars of free speech, they also wanted to ensure the online triumph of progressive speech. And that put them in a position that could only be contradictory, since a major, online anti-progressive revolt was using their platforms to successfully fight progressivism.

Adding to the confusion was the reality that Big Tech was forced to engage in two very different kinds of censorship.

The first kind was as old as the state itself. It involved the suppression of unwanted speech through the use of human censors. Big Tech corporate divisions, staffed by human beings (i.e., staffed by underpaid progressives) employed outside expert help (i.e., help from higher paid progressives), to make "judgments" about "problematic" texts and videos. These judgments were to be based upon an intellectual distinction between "freedom of speech" and the "abuse of freedom of speech," which meant that Big Tech could claim that they were not engaged in censorship at all, but were merely upholding "objective" standards when it came to publicly permissible speech. In other words, Big Tech was resurrecting the old major media claim that they were only "neutral" adjudicators of speech.

This claim was not very convincing to those who were being censored.

Also, given the huge number of texts and videos that were constantly being created online, a full regime of human censorship was clearly impossible. Such a project would have required the hiring of millions of people at a cost in the billions. Thus human censorship was usually limited to "major controversies." A "major controversy" occurred when a large number of people online publicly complained about some particular text or video. But this soon became a process that was socially engineered by progressive organizations, or by the major media, who provided "major public protests" as needed. However, it was the sheer subjectivity of human censorship that often resulted in bad publicity for Big Tech.

A second and more effective kind of censorship was by computer algorithm. However, using algorithms to decide what should be censored was also problematic, since algorithms are limited when it comes to questions of meaning. Still, in a rough kind of way, it did become possible for Big Tech to combine censorship by human beings with censorship by algorithms to create a hybrid censorship model, while still claiming to uphold "freedom of speech."

Also: If one begins with the conviction that progressive beliefs are an objective claim about the nature of reality, while anti-progressive beliefs are largely subjective opinion, it becomes possible, after a fashion, to "objectively" decide when anti-progressive speech should be banned or algorithmically downgraded. And since Big Tech is a major employer of recent college graduates, and since most recent college graduates are now taught from childhood, and fully believe, that there is no legitimate opposition to progressive beliefs, the decision of what to censor becomes easier over time.

Unlimited freedom of speech became a progressive dogma during the twentieth century, because that dogma served their interests. In that century, conflicts over freedom of speech almost invariably involved progressives publicly declaiming against censorship by non-progressive institutions. Therefore unlimited freedom of speech and the progressive revolution were always understood to be the same thing. However, now that progressives control all the major institutions of society, unlimited freedom of speech as a method for subverting the authority of institutions is now the political weapon of anti-progressives. This is why progressives are suddenly discovering the necessity for limits on that "unlimited freedom."

Indeed, progressives today argue that there is a radical distinction to be made between "freedom of speech" and something called "hate speech." Although progressives once believed unconditionally in freedom of speech, they now believe that "hate speech" should be banned. And just what, exactly, is "hate speech?" It is speech that is offensive to progressives.

One example of this can found in the recent public firing of James Damore from his job as a software engineer at Google. James Damore's crime was to participate in a company online memo on the problem of there being too few women software engineers at Google. Damore agreed that more needed to be done to actively recruit women, but then went on to argue that the company's stated goal of ensuring that half of all Google software engineers would be women ran up against the reality, demonstrated by many social scientific studies, that men and women have different interests and talents. Thus it was quite unlikely that half of all software engineers at Google would ever be women.

Needless to say, the progressive roof fell in on James Damore. He had violated a central progressive dogma, which is that there can be no substantive differences between men and women. Days of company-promoted, progressive hysteria immediately ensued. Not only was James Damore purged from his job, but so was anyone who dared to publicly defend him. Damore's common sense observations, backed by social scientific data, were completely unacceptable, not just to Google's progressive managers, but to organized groups of progressive witch-hunters within the company, who had been actively engaged for some time in harassing non-progressive employees. They not only publicly demanded that Damore be fired from Google, but demanded that he be subject to an industry-wide ban so as to ensure that he would never be able to work as a software engineer again.

In the joint lawsuit filed against Google by James Damore and Daniel Gudeman (another fired employee) one can find detailed accounts of the progressive witch hunts and public intimidation sessions that were a daily occurrence at Google even before Damore's firing. Intimidation by progressive Google managers, and by organized groups of progressive employees, had become the norm at Google. Google gave financial rewards to those employees who successfully sniffed out the witches in their midst.

This is Big Tech's vision of America's future.

Summary and Conclusion

I have tried, in this brief chapter, to trace the main lines of force within the current strategic situation.

Progressives now control every major institution in American life. The only real resistance to this progressive control of American society is to be found in the anti-progressive media, primarily online, which has arisen from nowhere to directly challenge progressive control of the news. The anti-progressive media are today the only real resistance to the progressive revolution.

The good news is that anti-progressives have managed to create an alternative to the dominant media and that alternative now reaches one third to one half of the American people. For the first time in modern American history, progressive control of the news is being publicly challenged.

The bad news is that the anti-progressive media remain outgunned. The old media, despite a radical collapse of market share, continue to have tens of millions of readers and viewers. The old media are also still the clearing house that defines the news in conjunction with the online progressive media. Most decisive of all, however, the progressive Big Tech platforms, through which most Americans now connect with each other online, are engaged in a major strategic effort to suppress the anti-progressive media on their platforms and on the Internet as a whole.

That is the current strategic situation.

Notes:

Details of the class action lawsuit filed against Google by the lawyers for James Damore. https://www.scribd.com/document/368688363/Jame s-Damore-vs-Google-Class-Action-Lawsuit

Here Are All The Media Outlets Blatantly Lying About The Google Memo by Bre Payton, The Federalist, August 8, 2017. An overview of the major media lies about the Damore memo. http://thefederalist.com/2017/08/08/media-outlets-blatantly-lying-google-memo/

19 Insane Tidbits From James Damore's Lawsuit About Google's Office Environment by Rachel Stoltzfoos, The Federalist, January 10, 2018. An overview of incidents described in the Damore lawsuit, detailing the pervasive political and social coercion that is part of the Google work experience.
http://thefederalist.com/2018/01/10/19-insane-tidbits-james-damores-lawsuit-googles-office-environment/

Immediate Strategies

Although the only strategic battle that is currently being waged against progressivism comes from the anti-progressive media online, the progressive control of American society cannot be destroyed merely by overthrowing their control of the news.

A universal replacement of progressive institutions is required.

That replacement will take place in two steps. First, there will be immediate software strategies that will undermine the major Big Tech platforms. Second, there will be long term software strategies that will radically decentralize the political and social order.

In this chapter, we will analyze the immediate software strategies that are already creating alternatives to the Big Tech platforms. Unfortunately, all such strategies face a current common difficulty. Although there are many good alternatives to the Big Tech platforms already in existence, the general public is not moving to those alternatives.

There are two major reasons for this.

First, the Big Tech platforms are both widely used and widely understood by the general public. They are now the way in which most Americans interact with one another online. Thus simple inertia dictates that most Americans will remain on the Big Tech platforms. It is an old commercial rule of thumb that most people will continue to use the products with which they are familiar unless you can create a product that is ten times better. Unfortunately, most of the alternatives to the Big Tech platforms are not as sophisticated as those platforms, let alone an order of magnitude better.

Second, there is a major problem in that the average American is largely unconcerned about Big Tech's unceasing surveillance of his online words and actions.

If, four generations ago, you had predicted that the Americans of the future would voluntarily submit to a complete surveillance and recording of everything that they said and did simply to get "free online services," no one would have been believed your prediction. No "real American" ever would submit to that kind of surveillance.

However, most Americans today take the view that, because they are not criminals, they have nothing to hide. They simply do not take seriously the threat of this unceasing, permanently recorded surveillance of their actions and words. The reality is that every American is now liable to blackmail, since everyone has secrets they don't want others to know. And since progressives are now dedicated to programs of social coercion and intimidation, soon every American will be guilty of thought-crimes for which they easily can be blackmailed.

There is also this: the average American of today at least claims to believe that nothing can be done about this ongoing technological surveillance. But while it is certainly true that nothing can any longer be done through the democratic process, or through the legal system, there is a universe of technological alternatives to much of this surveillance. If these alternatives were embraced by a majority of Americans, the worst of that surveillance would be curtailed. And the adoption of these alternatives would also spur the creation of further alternatives.

The average American is not interested.

But there is a minority of Americans, numbering at least in the tens of millions, who are actively seeking to escape Big Tech's surveillance and the surveillance of the national security state. This why there are alternatives to the Big Tech platforms.

These alternatives are of two kinds.

First, there are alternatives that can be used by advanced computer users. For most people, these alternatives are much too complicated to master or to use. For example, it is possible to replace your computer operating system (which is controlled by either Microsoft or Apple) with some version of the Linux operating system. Although the latest iterations of Linux are vastly simpler and easier to use than in the past, this remains a step too far for the average user. In this essay, we will ignore this group of alternatives, because advanced computer users will already know about them.

Second, there are alternatives for the average computer user. We will briefly list and describe some of those alternatives below, although we will avoid the whole smartphone problem in order to keep that analysis short.

Alternatives to Google and Bing

duckduckgo.com
startpage.com

Unlike Google and Bing, these search engines do not track their users. They do not identify your computer, they do not place cookies on your browser, and they keep no records of your searches. They make money by placing a limited number of ads on your immediate search results.

Duckduckgo is a complete search engine. However, unlike Google, it does not list every possible website in response to your query. It specializes in focusing on a limited number of sites that are the most likely to have an answer to that query.

Startpage acts as an intermediary between you and Google. It allows you to do Google searches without Google being able to identify you, track you, or record you. It delivers no information to Google about you. Startpage also provides a free proxy service that allows you to visit webpages on their search results without those sites being able to identify or to track you.

One drawback to Startpage is that, since it uses Google, many anti-progressive webpages will have been purged from the Google results or are found much later in those results.

Alternatives to Facebook and Twitter

gab.ai
minds.com

Gab is the primary alternative to Twitter. As of January 2018, gab had 375,000 users (compared to Twitter's 330 million). Gab considers itself to be the free speech version of Twitter and has few restrictions on content, whether text or video. Although open to all, Gab has become the destination site for anti-progressives who are being censored, banned, or who have had their content downgraded on Twitter.

Minds.com is the primary alternative to Facebook. As of January 2018, Minds had over two million active users (compared to Facebook's 2 billion). Minds is also an alternative to Twitter and YouTube. It uses end-to-end encryption on its website, as well as asymmetrically encrypted chat messaging, to protect user privacy. Nothing that you say or do on Minds will be seen by anyone except with your permission.

Recently, Google banned Minds.com from buying ads on Google's search engine results, as well as on the thousands of websites that run Google ads. Although Google is not in direct competition with Minds, except in the limited sense that Minds hosts videos, there is a strategic reason why Google wants to throttle Minds' growth. Minds is a major alternative platform where people are not spied upon. And that is not behavior that Google wants to encourage. Together with Facebook, which is Minds' chief rival, Google wants a universal, progressive surveillance regime.

Alternatives to YouTube

bitchute.com
minds.com

Google's YouTube is currently engaged in a major strategic campaign of demonetization, search downgrading, and the outright banning of anti-progressive videos. This campaign includes the deletion of the video archives of banned videographers, so that they cannot be recovered. This assault has led many videomakers to move their work from YouTube to other video online services or to duplicate their YouTube archives on other services in the event that they are finally banned by YouTube.

YouTube is the world's largest and best video platform. More than half a million hours of new videos are uploaded to that platform every day.

There are three major reasons why YouTube dominates online video.

First, if you want your video to be seen by the entire world, you will want to upload it to YouTube. YouTube viewers number in the hundreds of millions.

Second, YouTube's interface and technical capabilities are superior to all the other online video services.

Third, Google is willing to lose at least two billion dollars a year for the privilege of being the world's video platform. Google is willing to lose that much money because their surveillance of everyone who posts or views YouTube videos is an essential part Google's overall strategic plan to know everything there is to know about everyone who is online.

Fourth, although there are a number of alternatives to YouTube, only a few of those alternatives are committed to not collecting information about their users and to not censoring the videos on their platforms. Unfortunately, only a handful approach the technical standards found on YouTube. BitChute and Minds are two platforms that stand out.

Minds, however, is primarily a social media site that also hosts videos. Thus it is not in direct competition with YouTube.

BitChute is a fully functional, decentralized, peer-to-peer video network. In one sense, it is technically superior to YouTube. Whenever you view a video on

BitChute you become part of the decentralized net-work. The video you watch is downloaded to your computer and your computer is used to "pass" the video on to others. In creating a radically decentralized network, based upon its users, BitChute avoids the huge expense of buying the necessary bandwidth and online storage necessary to house and transmit popular videos. Whenever large numbers of people request a particular video, everyone who downloads that video becomes part of the expanding network providing that video.

However, BitChute does not engage in any surveillance or recording of its users or videographers. Your "hosting" of any video is temporary and leaves no record.

An Alternative to Your Web Browser:

brave.com

Every one of the major web browsers are part of the Big Tech tracking regime. The mission of most browsers is to identify you and then to continually track you and record your movements. Although some users have added ad blockers to their browsers, this is a solution only to the problem of ads. It does not solve the prob-lem of tracking and recording.

The Brave browser does not track its users, although it does allow you to enable cookies when an individual website requires their use. Brave makes its money by allowing a small number of ads to be discreetly placed on websites that you visit. But Brave keeps no record of your browsing history.

Brave is also known for its unique, voluntary payments system by which a user can financially support websites of his choice. Brave allows the user to designate small, recurring payments to those websites.

An Alternative to Your Email Program:

protonmail.com

According to Forbes magazine, Protonmail is "The only email system the NSA can't access." Protonmail was originally developed by a group of scientists working for CERN (The European Organization of Nuclear Research), the largest particle research laboratory in the world. Hence the name Protonmail.

Protonmail is incorporated in Switzerland and all of its servers are located there. User data are protected by Swiss privacy laws.

According to the Protonmail website, "All emails are secured automatically with end-to-end encryption. This means even we cannot decrypt and read your emails. As a result, your encrypted emails cannot be shared with third parties."

The only drawback to Protonmail is that most of those who will receive your emails will not be using an encrypted email programs. So your emails will continue to be available to the general surveillance system, except when you communicate with those who are using either Protonmail or some other encrypted service.

When you create an email account, Protonmail does not require any personal information. And they keep no IP logs that can be linked to your account. Thus even a court order can reveal nothing about you, since Protonmail has no information about you.

Currently, Protonmail has over a million users worldwide.

The basic email account is free. Protonmail makes money by offering paid accounts at various levels of service, including accounts for organizations. The free account is limited to 150 messages per day, three folders for messages, and 500 MB of storage. Paid accounts start at five dollars per month.

Alternatives to Wikipedia:

everipedia.org
infogalactic.org

Wikipedia, one of the most visited websites in the world, can be quite useful except when it comes to information about politics or religion. Wikipedia then becomes little more than a progressive propaganda organ. Unfortunately, most alternatives to Wikipedia are inferior products. Everipedia and Infogalactic, however, are ambitious recent entries that may well succeed in becoming genuine alternatives. Because Wikipedia's content is not copyrighted, but under a creative commons license, both Everipedia and Infogalactic have ported all of Wikipedia's content to their sites and are engaged in a process of editing, and adding to, that content.

An Alternative to Amazon and EBay

OpenBazaar.org

OpenBazaar is a radically decentralized software system that is used for the buying and selling goods. You simply download the software to your computer and either open a store yourself or use the software to search for stores and products.

Because the software is solely under the control of anyone who downloads it, and because the software is not owned or controlled by anyone, but is an open source system, there are no transaction fees for buying or selling. Every sale takes place directly between particular buyers and sellers. Of course, this also means that there is no one responsible for guaranteeing that any particular buyer will actually provide the goods sold or that a particular seller will actually pay for those goods. However, there is an escrow system that you can pay for that holds payments until deliveries are confirmed. However, if you trust the seller, or the buyer, you are not required to use the escrow service.

Unfortunately, there is one feature of OpenBazaar that currently ensures that the average computer user will not soon be using the platform. All payments within the OpenBazaar system are made in cryptocurrencies, with Bitcoin being the default cryptocurrency.

The organization that created the software for OpenBazaar makes money by selling "add-ons" to merchants who want more sophisticated controls over their stores. In January 2018, forty thousand people were using OpenBazaar.

An Alternative to Siri, Alexa, and Google Assistant

Viv.ai

Currently, Apple's Siri, Amazon's Alexa, and Google Assistant are the big sellers in personal technology. However, these "personal assistants" are little more than personal spies. They soak up all the information they can about you and send it to Big Tech. No anti-progressives in their right minds will use Siri, Alexa, or Google Assistant. Unfortunately, tens of millions of Americans now use these services.

There are no current alternatives to these personal assistants, although there is one alternative system under construction. The original developers of Siri are engaged in a project called Viv. Viv is an open source platform that will be under the complete control of the individual user. The user alone will decide which sources of information he will use to answer his questions, and will also decide how much information about his use of Viv will be shared with others.

Unfortunately, Viv was recently purchased by Samsung, so it remains to be seen whether this level of privacy will be allowed in the future.

Summary and Conclusion

The immediate strategies listed above are necessary, but insufficient.

Even if the average American adopted most of these alternatives, Big Tech would still continue to possess enough online tools to continue its surveillance of most Americans. At the same time, however, a general adoption of these alternative platforms would be a major victory over Big Tech.

Unfortunately, a general adoption of these alternatives is unlikely. The average American is simply not interested.

Still. millions of Americans are in the process of adopting these platforms. And many of these platforms may well become the springboards to larger strategies that can finally destroy the Big Tech platforms. We now turn to an analysis of these larger strategies.

Urbit: Creating A New Internet

One way to radically decentralize the Internet is to create a completely new Internet. Urbit is the name of the project that is in the process of creating that new Internet.

How will Urbit accomplish this?

Those who are working on Urbit refer to it as a "personal server." Now a "server," as that computer term is usually understood, consists of a computer that is outside of your personal control. A server found somewhere on the Internet, for example, might provide you with a particular kind of services. For example, Facebook's servers both provide and control your experience with Facebook. None of those Facebook servers is under your control. Rather, Facebook controls them. And they not only provide the services that you expect from Facebook, but track and record everything that you do.

But Urbit is a personal server. What, exactly, does that mean?

Let us briefly engage in a thought experiment. Imagine that a single corporation buys up every service that people use online and then runs all those services from its own servers. Imagine, for example, Facebook buying up and controlling every service that you use online. Facebook will now own both Google and Amazon. It will own and control every other software service that you use. For example, it will now host the software that runs your bank account. And this Super-Facebook will track and record everything that you do in every one of those services. All your online postings and all your email messages are contained on the servers owned and controlled by Super-Facebook.

For all practical purposes, Super-Facebook has become the Internet. Everything that you do online runs on Facebook software and on Facebook servers, and, therefore, Facebook knows everything that there is to know about you. It would be like the Internet of today, only a single corporation would run everything.

Of course, today all of the services that you use online are split into dozens of computer clouds, software applications, and innumerable servers, run by very different corporations. You do not even know how many different online services you are using. Still, each of those services tracks and records what you do. The corporations who own these services – Facebook, Google, Amazon, and so on – also know a great deal about you. And behind those giant corporations is the American national security state, which also tracks and records everything that you do. That is today's Internet.

However, let us return to the concept of a single corporation running everything. And let us imagine that this corporation turns out to be a singularly selfless institution. The people who run this corporation are in love with human freedom. They think of little else. So they have decided not to track you or keep any data about you. Instead, they have come up with a brand new understanding of the Internet. They have created a free personal server for each person online. This personal server will be under each person's direct control. While the personal server can track you and record your movements, you alone will have access to this information. You alone will control the server.

Anyone who wants to provide a service must now come and ask you if they can be part of your "personal server." And they will have access to your personal server only to the extent that you permit them to have access. No data will be made available to them except the data that you decide to make available. No outside service will be able to track you or to know anything about you except to the extent that you decide to give them that knowledge.

This is, more or less, Urbit's definition of a "personal server."

In one sense, Urbit represents an attempted return to the Internet of the early nineties, before the era of graphical interfaces and web browsers. The few millions of people online in those days were only able to access other computers on the Internet through the use of a "command line." A computer screen in those days showed white text on a black background. And that was it. When you typed a command on your screen, this allowed you to "log on" to another computer somewhere on the Internet. And that computer was allowing you to "log on." Once you were "logged on" to that computer, you could type in further commands to maneuver "within" that distant computer's public menu. And that menu was fairly rudimentary. You could navigate it by using the up and down keys, after which you would hit "enter" to go to a particular choice. By this method, you could gain access to textual information or else download files. But you did not have access to anything on that distant computer other than what that distant computer allowed. You could access only those documents or files that the distant computer made publicly available.

Urbit is a hyper-sophisticated version of this kind of decentralized computing.

With your personal Urbit server, the online world now comes to you. You no longer shop at Amazon. The Amazon website has disappeared. Amazon now comes to you. If you send a message to Amazon, and to a list of other online book sellers, telling them that you are looking for a particular book, Amazon and those other sellers will submit descriptions and bids to you. You can automate your software so that you do not have to deal with the bids yourself. The software sets the details of the physical condition of the book and the price that you will pay. The software will buy the book.

Suppose you want to set up a "Facebook page." But Facebook no longer exists. Instead, you will use your own software to create a "personal page" or several different kinds of personal pages. You will have one for close friends and family, one for mild acquaintances, one for customers, and one for the public at large. Anyone who visits these pages will visit them through your personal server. All of your interactions with those who visit those pages will take place within your personal server. Thus all the information about those interactions will be known only to you and to those with whom you are interacting. No one else will have that information.

Facebook is gone. There is no Facebook.

Or take your current email program. Today, most Americans have one or more email accounts. Those accounts are invariably outside of the user's control. Almost all of our emails, as well as all of your replies to emails, are in the possession of the corporations who track and record all of your interactions, and compile data profiles from them.

With Urbit, all of your email accounts are managed by you through an encrypted email server, which is part of your personal server. All of the communications found in those emails, whether sent or received, are known only to you and to those with whom you correspond. No third party sees them, tracks them, or records them.

Are you beginning to see the outlines of a radically new Internet?

How does Urbit work?

Given the monumental technological complexity of the Internet, as well as the huge sunk costs that have gone into creating it, how is it even possible to think of creating a completely new Internet? Who would even pay for such a thing?

Urbit's radical answer to this question is that the Urbit protocol "runs on top" of the current Internet. Urbit will exist as a layer over the existing Internet software. It will manipulate that software, but will be completely separate from it. Since there is no direct connection between the Urbit protocol and the current Internet protocol, no one will be able to "hack" into the Urbit protocol from the existing Internet.

Today, we have separate software systems for every-thing that we do. For instance, there is software that runs the Internet, there is software that runs your personal computer, there is software that runs your email program, and there is software that runs other programs on your computer. All of these are com-pletely unrelated programs that have to work together. And this is why computer hacking and computer viruses are so common. To make all these programs work together requires software "patches" between them that inevitably contain innumerable "holes" in that software that can be exploited.

Urbit largely solves the hacking and virus problems because it is a single software system. It is simultaneously an Internet operating system, a computer operating system, an email program, and the software into which all your other programs are plugged. Different programs no longer have to be engineered to work together. Every key software program is part of the single software program called Urbit.

Today, most personal computers run either on the Windows or Apple operating systems. These operating systems are constructed of millions of lines of code. They are highly complex systems that allow programmers to create other software programs that are then able to interact with these operating systems.

When finished, Urbit is expected to contain only thirty thousand lines of code, not millions of lines. Urbit is a vast simplification. It is a radically new kind of coding.

In the words of Galen Wolfe-Pauly, the CEO of Tlon, the parent company of Urbit:

> Urbit is a complete, clean-slate system software stack: a non-lambda interpreter (Nock), a functional language (Hoon), and an event-driven OS (Arvo), with its own encrypted protocol (Ames), typed revision control (Clay), reactive web server (Eyre) and functional build system (Ford). The full system, including basic apps, is only 30,000 lines of Hoon.

One of the more radical things that Urbit accomplishes is to create a system of online identities that are specific to the individuals who own those identities. Although being anonymous online will still be possible, it will be possible only under very limited circumstances.

Currently, an "Internet identity" is the identity of the computer or device that you use to connect to the Internet. People do not have Internet identities; machines do. Urbit ends this system. Although computers and devices will continue to have online identities, the main online identities will belong to human beings. With Urbit, when you use a computer or other device to access the Internet, you will use your personal identity to gain access, no matter what device you are using. And since all online communications will be encrypted, with each individual possessing an encrypted key to his own personal identity, no one will be able to steal your personal identity and falsely masquerade as you, unless he steals that key.

How close is Urbit to launching?

This essay is being written in early 2018. Although the testing of the essential elements of Urbit has taken place, the program is nowhere near launch. Individual programs that work within Urbit are limited in number. And this number will remain limited until after Urbit publicly launches, which will then give developers an incentive to create those programs. Urbit will probably not launch until next year.

The chief engineers of Urbit are more interested in perfecting Urbit than in making it publicly available. Given the magnitude of their task, even after launch the plan is for a very gradual adoption of Urbit by the general public. The expectation is that the public rollout may last for several years, after which they expect Urbit to become the new Internet.

Who controls the Urbit system?

Urbit is currently a highly centralized software operation. However, this will last only until the public launch. At that point, Urbit will become a radically de-centralized system by deliberate design. There will be no centralized control of the Urbit software. No one will "own" Urbit. Instead, everyone will own their own personal Urbit.

Won't software updates to the Urbit code be a form of centralized control?

There is no such thing as a software program that is perfect, finished, or unhackable. Therefore Urbit will require software updates in response to events. This reality alone precludes any attempt to create a fully decentralized system of code governance. Those who are in charge of updating the Urbit code will, in essence, control Urbit.

The problem of centralized power returns.

But the creators of Urbit believe that they have found a solution to this problem. The Urbit code will begin by instantiating a federal system of code control. When it comes to code governance, Urbit will be a digital republic.

If you have an identity within the Urbit system you will belong to one of three classes of users. These classes are called Galaxies, Stars, and Planets. The average Urbit user will own a planet. Every planet will belong to a star and every star will belong to a galaxy. This is not only the format of Urbit governance, but is the formal Urbit network. Urbit is being engineered to support over four billion individual planet identities, grouped under the classes of stars and galaxies.

There is an upper limit of 256 galaxy class identities and an upper limit of 65,536 star identities (or 256 stars per galaxy). There will be 65,536 planets per star, which adds up to a little over four billion planets.

The average user of Urbit – a planet – will have no input into changes of computer code, except for the ability to leave one star for another if they do not like the code governance exercised by their previous star. This right to secede is a fundamental part of the Urbit code. Stars have the same relationship to galaxies. They can change galaxies if they are dissatisfied with the galaxy to which they belong. But it is galaxies and stars alone who constitute the "upper and lower houses" of Urbit code governance. They alone possess the ability to change the Urbit code. And those changes will be made by consensus rather than by vote. Those who do not agree with the consensus can secede to create their own system within the tripartite Urbit structure.

In short, Urbit is not a fully decentralized system. But it is a radically decentralized federal system.

As to the question of how those who are creating Urbit intend to get make money on this project, the answer is: by selling real estate. Most of the galaxies, stars, and planets will be sold as property to the general public. Urbit may very well become the new Internet.

Notes:

Urbit is currently very low key in informing the public of its progress. Most of the provided information tends toward the technical and thus is of interest primarily to programmers.

The place to begin to learning about Urbit is at: **urbit.org**. Currently, **fora.urbit.org/updates** provides weekly information on the project. Also: you can get an overview of the system at **urbit.org/docs**.

For videos dealing with Urbit that are made by those who are involved in it, search on YouTube for "Mars Talk (Urbit)" or search for "Joshua Reagan." Currently, no new videos are being produced.

On Epicenter, an online technology interview show, there is an early 2018 interview with Galen Wolfe-Pauley, CEO of Tlon, the company that is creating Urbit. The video is at: **epicenter.tv/episode/205**.

Smart Contracts: Merging Agreement and Execution

What is a smart contract?

It is a contract that merges "agreement and execution." But what, exactly, does that mean?

Take a normal contract between two parties. That contract will generally be a written agreement that requires the parties to it to undertake certain actions in order to "execute" the contract. When those actions take place the contract is completed. There will be no problems so long as both of the parties agree that it has been properly executed. But if they do not agree, then a third party must then be brought in to "interpret" the contract and to enforce this interpretation upon the parties. Ultimately, this means recourse to the courts.

A smart contract eliminates all third party interpretation of contracts, including courts of law. It does this by eliminating the possibility of interpretation. By merging "agreement and execution" there is literally nothing for anyone to interpret, since a smart contract is a contract that is self-executing.

How can a contract be self-executing?

To explain how a smart contract works the metaphor of a vending machine is sometimes used. If you put money into a vending machine, the machine responds by releasing the item that you have selected, along with any change that is owed to you. In other words, "agreement" (the insertion of your money into the machine) and "execution" (the selected item is released along with any change due to you) becomes a single operation. Agreement and execution have been merged. But there is one major difference between a vending machine and a smart contract. Smart contract are guaranteed to execute, while vending machines sometimes refuse to do so.

So how does a smart contract merge agreement and execution? And how is it possible to guarantee that a smart contract will always execute?

Here is one definition of a smart contract: "A smart contract is decentralized [computer] code that moves money based upon a condition."[1] When that condition is met, the code will be executed, since it is impossible for the code not to execute once the condition is met. Also: a smart contract can be set up as a series of decentralized codes, with each piece of code releasing money when that part of the contract has been fulfilled. It is even possible to create multiple smart contracts that will interact with each other as a complex set of decentralized codes, releasing money when parts of those contracts have been fulfilled.

When one of the conditions of a smart contract has been fulfilled, the parties to the contract use their "digital signatures" to signal to the contract that they agree that the condition has been fulfilled. It is these digital signatures that will trigger the smart contract to release the money tied to the execution of that condition.

There is another important aspect to smart contracts. Before the money is released by a smart contract it is being held "in escrow" by the smart contract itself. One way a smart contract can "hold" money is by using a cryptocurrency such as Bitcoin. Because Bitcoin is computer code, the Bitcoin code (or some other cryptocurrency code) can be embedded within the smart contract. This money then becomes part of the computer code that makes up the smart contract. When the condition for the money's release occurs, the smart contract code is automatically programmed to reassign the ownership of the money from the smart contract to whoever is authorized by the contract to receive that money.

Now it is possible for a smart contract to release money that is being held in escrow by a bank or some other financial institution. But this would mean that the release of money takes place outside of the smart contract itself. And that would mean that a third party, in this case the financial institution holding that money, would be in control of that money. In a full smart contract, however, all third parties are eliminated, which means that a full smart contract will contain an embedded cryptocurrency.

Once a smart contract is set in motion, no party to the contract any longer has control over its execution. Nor can any third party interfere in that smart contract's execution, including the courts. All that can now happen is that the parties to the smart contract will certify, using their digital signatures, that certain conditions of the smart contract have been fulfilled, after which money is released by that contract.

With the exception of two states, today's American legal system does not yet treat smart contracts as genuine contracts. It does not matter. A smart contract is binding whether it is legal or not. Nor is it possible for any court to "interpret" the "meaning" of a smart contract, since the contract can only be executed according to the code embedded in it. This is all the "meaning" that a smart contract has. Even if a court "orders" a smart contract to be "interpreted" to mean something different from what the code executes, such a decision still does not matter. It does not matter because no court can actually alter the code that is embedded in the smart contract. All that a court can do is to order the parties to a smart contract to not obey it.

Why is the code in a smart contract unbreakable?

A smart contract becomes unbreakable when it is embedded on something called a blockchain. We will deal with the blockchain in the next essay. Here we will point out that if you have nearly unlimited resources it is possible to alter computer code found on a blockchain. However, for most purposes, for most people, and for most of the time, it is impossible to alter computer code embedded on a blockchain.

All that we need to know for the moment is that, for all practical purposes, a smart contract embedded on a blockchain is incapable of being altered. Once again: a judge could declare that a particular smart contract is illegal. He may order the parties to the contract to be put in jail if they use their digital signatures to proceed to carry out that smart contract. But the smart contract itself will only execute according to the code embedded on the blockchain.

At some point in the future, our legal system will come to recognize that smart contracts cannot be interpreted by judges. It will also recognize that the only practical way to ensure that illegal smart contracts are not created will be to vet such contracts before they are placed on a blockchain. However, once a smart contract is embedded on a blockchain, it will be independent of all third party interventions, including the inter- ventions of judges.

Therefore the lawyers of the future who draw up smart contracts will need a radically new kind of legal training. For one thing, they will have to know how to write computer code. At the same time, legal simplicity will become a dominant feature of smart contracts, since most smart contracts will be variations of established templates.

This brings us to another important aspect of smart contracts. Legally, a smart contract can function as an "independent, verifiable middle-man."[2]

The reason why we have large corporations in the modern era is because the corporate form is the most efficient way to organize large, complex economic activities.

Take the mass production of cars for example. In theory, it is possible to mass produce cars by hiring many independent subcontractors for each step in the car assembly process. But we know from experience that it is impossible to mass produce cars using this system. To assemble each one of the hundreds of parts of a car into a whole requires that each part be physically present at the precise time that it needs to be added to the car's assembly. It is simply impossible to organize that kind of manufacturing precision unless those who are assembling the car become employees under the direct control of a single employer. If the mass production of cars were to be done by independent contractors, a single contractor that failed to do his job, for whatever reason, would shut down the entire line. Thus organizational reality dictates that mass-assembly line workers have to be employees controlled by a hierarchical system.

But this will not be true in the future.

Smart contracts can become "middlemen" that will allow groups of independent contractors to mass produce products and services. Even today, there are complicated businesses, such as the movie-making business, or construction firms, where a large number of independent contractors are temporarily assembled and directed by a managerial team for the length of a particular contract. The "middle man" in these cases is the management company that hires and oversees the subcontractors. However, in the future, entire projects will be "run" by the smart contract itself. Each contractor on a project will deal directly with the smart contract. The smart contract will specify the actions that the contractor must take and when those actions must be executed. And there will be no arguments over the proper "interpretation" of that contract, since agreement and execution are the same event.

In the future, there will be major corporations that have no employees. The temporary mass production of a particular car style, for example, might be organized as a series of smart contracts. Once that particular "car project" has been completed, the contract will be terminated.

This new kind of organization has a name. It is called a DAO or Decentralized Autonomous Organization.[3] Smart contracts will eventually disintermediate most businesses and industries by becoming the "middle-man" that will "run" these Decentralized Autonomous Organizations. Now there are many people who are likely to react negatively to this idea. After all, a smart contract sounds like a pretty unforgiving instrument of control. It refuses to be interpreted and is guaranteed to execute no matter what anyone says or does. A smart contract thus may appear to be more threatening than liberating.

In reality, it is our present system of contract law that is the more threatening.

All of today's contractual relationships are guaranteed by third parties, who get to "interpret" those contracts in ways that the parties who agreed to those contracts never intended. And today's contracts are, to a great degree, successfully "interpreted" by those with the most money and legal expertise to enforce the contract in a way that favors their interests. Because of this, contracts are written in an attempt to nail down every last detail of an agreement as a way to ensure that no one who is a party to that contract can get the upper hand.

Thus, as anyone who has ever purchased a house knows, the "closing" can be a real pain. Take merely the "title" to the house. Not only must a specialized and bonded human being, from an agency, investigate to ensure that it is clear of all legal impediments, but the systems of title registration and validation are so corrupted that you must also have title insurance just in case something later pops up that this investigation did not reveal. And that's just the title.

However, if you had title registration on a blockchain, no title could be registered at all that was not provably a clear title – provable within the code itself – while the transfer of that title would be a completely automatic process that would need no human interventions or research at all. Simply by having the complete history of any title on the blockchain, your title to the property that you are purchasing would be guaranteed.

Multiply this kind of legal simplicity across every form of contractual obligation. A smart contract on a blockchain means that it will no longer be possible for those with money and lawyers, or those trying to weasel out of contractual obligations, to take control of the process. The smart contract will simply execute as designed. The result is guaranteed because the result cannot be otherwise. The enforcement of a smart contract is enabled within the smart contract itself, because it is embedded on a blockchain.

All that you need to do is to get the smart contract right in the first place.

Notes:

1. *Ethereum: blockchains, digital assets, smart contracts, decentralized autonomous organizations* by Henning Diedrich (2016), 167.

2. Diedrich, 171.

3. Diedrich, 180-186.

The Blockchain: Establishing Relationships without Trust

Let us briefly review the idea of smart contracts.

In a regular contract, the parties agree to undertake specific actions to bring about a contract's execution. And there will be no problems as long as the parties agree that they have acted as the contract specifies. But if they disagree, a third party must then be brought in to interpret that contract and to enforce that interpretation upon the parties. Of course, the ultimate third party is a court of law.

Smart contracts, however, abolish all such third party interpretations through the simple expedient of eliminating interpretation. The whole point of a smart contract is that it merges "agreement and execution." To agree to a smart contract is the same thing as to execute that smart contract, since agreement and execution are single event, written directly into the computer code. Like a vending machine, a smart contract automatically executes when you put it in motion. Unlike a vending machine, a smart contract is never prone to mechanical error. It will always execute as written.

Thus no courts are needed to enforce smart contracts. When a smart contract is set into motion it becomes (almost) unstoppable. It will always execute as written. However, a smart contract is not a computer program as such. Nor is it a legal text "expressed" as a computer program. A smart contract is actual computer code which engineers "agreement and execution" so that they are the same event.

Now when we say that a smart contract is (nearly) unstoppable, what do we mean by that? We mean is that if you throw enough computer resources at a smart contract it can be stopped. Although a court, for example, can declare that some particular smart contract is illegal, that alone is not enough to stop the smart contract from executing. If the smart contract is embedded on a blockchain it can never be stopped unless the entire blockchain is stopped from executing. And a blockchain can only be stopped at a huge cost to whoever is willing to expend the resources to stop it. Because it will almost always be much more expensive to stop a blockchain than to continue with a particular smart contract on that chain, smart contracts are – for all practical purposes – unstoppable.

One thing that makes a smart contract unstoppable is that it "owns" the money that is disbursed as the conditions of the contract are met. In the execution of the contract there will be a set number of events that must necessarily occur in a certain order. The parties to the contract must jointly agree that those events have occurred by using their digital signatures to signal to the smart contract that they agree that that event has occurred. At that point, some of the cryptocurrency embedded in the smart contract will be released to one of the parties. But if the parties do not agree that the contract has been properly executed, the smart contract will not release the money. And no more steps in the contract can be taken until agreement on that particular point is reached.

A smart contract can also disburse money that is deposited in a bank or some other financial institution, rather than having an embedded cryptocurrency as part of the smart contract. But that would mean that the money was being controlled by a third party outside of the smart contract. That third party could then dictate whether or not the contract was being properly executed. Thus a genuine smart contract will always have a cryptocurrency embedded within its code so that money that is disbursed will be completely controlled by the smart contract itself.

The primary reason why a smart contract can act independently of the parties to that contract, as well as independently of any third party interventions, is because it is imbedded on a blockchain.

What, exactly, is a blockchain?

There are several definitions of a blockchain. Most of the definitions are not so much wrong as they are incomplete. One incomplete definition is that a blockchain is a "distributed ledger." But although a blockchain is a distributed ledger, it is much more than that.

Let us begin with the word "blockchain." The "block" in the blockchain is a block of code. The blocks of code are then "chained together" to form the blockchain.

The blocks of code do not necessarily have to have anything to do with each other. For example, we might find two smart contracts on the same blockchain that have no relationship to each other at all, except that they are both found on the same blockchain.

So why, if they have no relationship to each other, are they are found on the same blockchain? They are found together because a blockchain exists to guarantee that smart contracts will not be altered. Everything that is found on a blockchain, whether smart contracts, digital records, computer programs, or any other form of code, have been "frozen" in their current form and can never be altered. The more data on a blockchain, the harder it becomes to alter anything on the blockchain. Thus any information that you do not want to be altered should be placed on a blockchain.

Now it is possible to create a smart contract that is not on a blockchain. However, in that case there is no guarantee that the contract cannot be altered. You could trust some third party, say a public or private institution, to guard your smart contract's code under a physical lock and key. But that guarantee rests on trusting the third parties. The whole point of a blockchain is to create a "trustless" guarantee in which there are no third parties. It is the blockchain which guarantees that the smart contract cannot be altered.

So if a blockchain guarantee is not based on trust, what is it based upon?

First, thousands of copies of a particular blockchain are distributed to thousands of computers around the world. If someone tries to alter even one of those copies, or many of them, the thousands of other copies will "recognize" that those copies have been altered and the altered copies will automatically be kicked out of the blockchain network.

This recognition is accomplished by embedding something called a "consensus protocol" into each copy of the blockchain. The consensus protocol ensures that, if someone alters even one iota of information found in that copy of the blockchain, it will be easy to discover that this has occurred. On every occasion in which all the copies of the blockchain are updated, the consensus protocol checks to ensure that every copy is exactly the same. Thus to successfully alter a blockchain means that you must have the ability to alter a majority of the thousands of copies in existence, since the majority rules when deciding which of the copies is the true copy. And such a mass forgery is nearly impossible to accomplish.

Blockchain expert Henning Diedrich:

> Because everyone [who has a copy of the blockchain] has all the data, everybody can check the validity of every single change in the world state [of the blockchain], and so therefore, nobody can cheat and pretend something that is not true.[1]

But how, exactly, does this work?

A blockchain is constructed so that every subsequent block that is added to the chain will embed a crypto-graphic "hash" of the block immediately preceding it. This hash consists of a coded mathematical calculation that cannot be read by anyone (since it is encrypted) and which contains a compressed version of all the information found in the previous block. And since each block that is added to the chain contains a cryptographic "hash" of every block that precedes it, the last block in any blockchain will always contain what amounts to a cryptographic "hash" of the infor-mation found in the entire chain. Thus if anything is altered in any block in the chain, the final hash of the final block of the chain will be completely different from the final hash that is found in the majority of the copies that make up the rest of the blockchain network. This constitutes "proof" that this particular copy has been corrupted. The copy is then automatically removed from the blockchain network.[2]

The longer the blockchain, and the further back in the chain that a particular block happens to be, the more impossible it becomes to alter either that particular block or the blockchain as a whole.

Bitcoin is an example of how this works, since Bitcoin is the Bitcoin blockchain.

Currently, Bitcoin is the world's most famous block-chain. And the Bitcoin blockchain exists to guarantee that Bitcoins cannot be altered or counterfeited. The Bitcoin blockchain also exists to guarantee that the ownership of a particular Bitcoin cannot be changed except through following the procedures that are embedded within the blockchain itself for the verification of that transfer of ownership. The Bitcoin blockchain records every transaction and change of ownership of every single Bitcoin in existence. In other words, the Bitcoin blockchain contains within itself the complete transactional history of every Bitcoin.

The Bitcoin blockchain is also constructed to ensure that there will be thousands of computers around the world who will want to maintain the thousands of copies of the Bitcoin blockchain without corrupt alteration. It ensures this by making it profitable to process Bitcoin transactions. The blockchain itself pays people to process Bitcoin transactions and ownership transfers, and to update the copies of the blockchain. And these people are paid in Bitcoins. The Bitcoin blockchain has been deliberately constructed so as to gradually release new Bitcoins into the system over time to pay for those services. Those who are engaged in processing the Bitcoin blockchain for profit are called "Bitcoin miners." They "mine" Bitcoin.

Today there are huge Bitcoin computer operations in China that do nothing more than "mine" Bitcoins for profit. These huge operations help to guarantee that the thousands of copies of the Bitcoin blockchain will remain in existence and that all Bitcoin transactions and ownership transfers will take place as guaranteed. Some analysts worry that too much of that computing power is now located behind the "Great Firewall of China" and that someday the Chinese might be able to take control of the Bitcoin blockchain. However, this is not yet a problem. And even if this were to occur, it is not entirely clear why it would be in the economic interest of the Chinese to subvert the source of their ongoing profits.

Probably the best known blockchain today, other than Bitcoin, is the online community called Ethereum. Those who are involved in Ethereum are interested in creating a radically decentralized society within the Ethereum blockchain. The Ethereum blockchain exists not only to host its own cryptocurrency, which is called "Ether," but to host smart contracts and other de-centralized software projects. These projects include attempts to create decentralized stock exchanges and decentralized banks that no one can own, since they are simply smart contracts on the Ethereum blockchain.

How many people and organizations are currently on the Ethereum blockchain? In mid-January of 2018, Ethereum was processing more than a million trans-actions a day, which is the closest one can come in estimating the number of users on the Ethereum blockchain.[3] And Ether is currently the second most valuable cryptocurrency in the world after Bitcoin. However, since the Ethereum blockchain is radically decentralized, all forms of cryptocurrency are used there. We will discuss Ethereum at greater length in a later chapter.

Although blockchains have been heralded as the next great revolution in technology, there are a number of major problems that have to be addressed before they become widely used.

A primary problem is that blockchains contain huge repositories of data. Take Bitcoin as an example. Although Bitcoin is the best known cryptocurrency, and the most widely used, it remains little more than a niche currency market. Just a few millions of people own Bitcoins. Now the chief problem standing in the way of Bitcoin's becoming a widely used currency is the length of time that it takes to complete a transaction on the Bitcoin blockchain. Each time there is a transaction, every copy of the thousands of copies of the blockchain on thousands of computers around the world must be updated and verified. And since each copy is a record of every transaction that has ever occurred on the blockchain, this requires a large amount of computer processing power.

Common credit card transactions, on the other hand, are simple to execute. The amount of information that is sent back and forth to confirm that your credit card is good is very limited. The average credit card company currently processes about 2,000 transactions per second, with an ability to reach peaks of 50,000 transactions. Bitcoin currently processes just 10 transactions per second. And that is a major problem.

There is another major problem. If Bitcoin suddenly became a major currency tomorrow, the amount of processing power that would be required to run its transactions would require the use of all the electricity currently being produced on earth.

This is also a showstopper.

Now there are a number of software projects that are working on solutions to these problems. But so far they have had only a limited success. The blockchain as it exists is not yet ready for prime time.

There is, however, a great deal of interest in block-chains in the financial community. Many of the world's largest banks and financial institutions are in the process of developing their own, private blockchains. They understand that a blockchain can guarantee the safety and security of financial transactions. They also understand that blockchains will enable them to process transactions with many fewer employees.

The big banks are also experimenting with blockchains in the hope that their business model, as third party intermediaries, will continue to exist in the age of blockchains. However, the logic of the blockchain is to do away with all third parties. Since the future of banking probably consists of smart contracts drawn up by individual lenders and borrowers, dealing directly with each other, without the necessity of banks, the banking industry's interest in this new technology is simply speeding up the process of their own dissolution.

Notes:

1. *Ethereum: blockchains, digital assets, smart contracts, decentralized autonomous organizations* by Henning Diedrich (2016), 113.

2. Diedrich, 112-123.

3. etherscan.io/chart/tx.

Cryptocurrencies: Decentralizing Money

What is a cryptocurrency?

A cryptocurrency is digital money that is embedded as cryptographic code on a blockchain.

The blockchain guarantees that the cryptocurrency cannot be counterfeited. It also guarantees that ownership of the cryptocurrency cannot be transferred except through unalterable procedures that are also embedded on the blockchain.

Since it is on a blockchain, the cryptocurrency is under no one's control. Since it obeys rules that are permanently embedded in the cryptocurrency blockchain, the cryptocurrency cannot be inflated or counterfeited. Each time that a cryptocurrency is used for a transaction the thousands of copies of the blockchain around the world are immediately synchronized to show that a transfer of ownership has occurred. This guarantees that, if some of the copies of the blockchain are illegally altered to show that something else happened, those copies will be identified and banned from the network.

One of the primary benefits of using cryptocurrencies, instead of government currencies, is that a crypto-currency can be permanently engineered so that there will never be inflation. If the total amount of a crypto-currency that is to be issued is embedded in the blockchain itself, and that total amount is publicly verifiable, then no inflation can occur. Inflation is always the product of governments who deliberately increase the amount of money in circulation so that each unit of that money becomes worth less over time. It is useful for governments to create inflation so that they can pay off their debts in money that is not worth as much as the money that they originally borrowed.

Thus inflation is always a hidden tax. It is also a tax that has bankrupted whole societies. This is one reason why cryptocurrencies are superior to government currencies, since cryptocurrencies can be deliberately engineered so that there is no inflation.

In the case of Bitcoin, the total number of Bitcoins that will eventually be issued is publicly known and embedded on the blockchain. Since the total number of Bitcoins will never exceed that amount, inflation cannot occur.

Of course, currently, the value of a Bitcoin fluctuates wildly from day to day. However, this is not the result of inflation, but of speculation. Today, no one knows whether Bitcoin is destined to become the world's primary cryptocurrency or whether Bitcoin will be displaced by some other cryptocurrency. Thus Bitcoin's value wildly fluctuates as people buy and sell it, because they are speculating on its future. They are also speculating on how much Bitcoin will be worth tomorrow. At this point in time, all cryptocurrencies are speculative, because the concept is new and untested. Cryptocurrencies as a complete substitute for government currencies is an idea whose time has not yet come.

But it is likely that cryptocurrencies will someday replace government currencies. This is because governments misuse their power to create money not only to produce inflation, but to artificially ease or tighten the cost of lending money. Governments continually attempt to micro-manage their economies by the manipulation of their money. And the costs of those manipulations are never borne by the governments themselves, but by ordinary people who are forced to use government money.

Cryptocurrencies will end the government manipulation of money.

Today, the major governments are preparing for the coming age of digital money. But digital money is not the same thing as a cryptocurrency. Most proposals for government digital money are drawn to ensure that government digital money will not be embedded on a blockchain, since that would mean that the government would no longer be able to manipulate its money. Instead, most such proposals aim at outlawing paper money so that everyone will have to use the government's digital money. And this digital money will be as easy to manipulate as paper money. More importantly, once government money is made completely digital it can be used by the government to track every economic transaction that every one of its citizens makes. In other words, digital money ensures that there will be a permanent government surveillance and record of all economic transactions.

Thus digital money is the opposite of a cryptocurrency. Digital money is meant to ensure complete government oversight and control over everything that its citizens do with that money. Blockchain cryptocurrencies, on the other hand, exist to ensure that no one can know about or control any transaction, except the individuals engaged in the transaction.

Thus we are in a race to the future.

Either we will have completely decentralized, non-governmental blockchain cryptocurrencies as the basis of our economy or there will be completely centralized, government-controlled digital currencies in which every transaction is tracked and recorded by the state, and in which the state can continue to manipulate the currency. Now it may seem that government digital monies must inevitably become the norm, and cryptocurrencies outlawed, since government rules by force and can ensure that its system will become the norm. But this is by no means an inevitable outcome. With each year that passes in which blockchain cryptocurrencies grow and multiply, and with more and more people using them, the harder it will be for governments to abolish cryptocurrencies in favor of their digital money.

Today Bitcoin is the world's leading cryptocurrency. And Bitcoin is the Bitcoin blockchain. As a crypto-currency pioneer, Bitcoin has had more than its share of problems. The most dramatic have involved criminal arrests and prosecutions. However, it should be noted that these criminal activities have occurred outside of the Bitcoin blockchain itself.

For example, there have been spectacular Bitcoin thefts involving tens of millions of dollars, but with these thefts taking place off the blockchain. The thefts occurred because the Bitcoin code does not have to reside on a blockchain. It can be transferred to cryptocurrency exchanges, which allow people to engage in transactions outside the blockchain. These exchanges exist because it is currently easier to trade Bitcoins off-chain or to "store" your Bitcoins where they can be easily reached. However, since Bitcoin ownership cannot be guaranteed off the Bitcoin blockchain, the cryptocurrency currency exchanges are vulnerable to theft. Because they are computerized, and centralized, they can be hacked. As with anything new, and particularly with a new form of money, such problems are inevitable.

Today, there are many other cryptocurrencies besides Bitcoin. The second most valuable cryptocurrency after Bitcoin is called Ether. However, the Ethereum blockchain is more than simply a cryptocurrency blockchain. Ethereum is a large community of people who are involved in using smart contracts to create a decentralized community online. And although Ether is the primary currency used on the Ethereum blockchain, since Ethereum is radically decentralized community any cryptocurrency can be used there.

Now today's cryptocurrencies are minor players in relation to the governmental currencies that currently dominate the world. At this point, few people own Bitcoins or any other cryptocurrency. But the total worth of cryptocurrencies is growing. Here is a list of the world's top five cryptocurrencies, and their value in American dollars, as of January 2018:

Bitcoin	$240 billion
Ethereum	$120 billion
Ripple	$82 billion
Bitcoin Cash	$44 billion
Cardano	$20 billion

We are only at the beginning of the cryptocurrency revolution.

Notes:

An overview of how cryptocurrencies work can be found in *The Internet of Money* by Andreas Antonopolis (2016). Also, see his online videos.

Ethereum: Creating the Decentralized Society

Ethereum is a community-driven project aiming to de-centralize the Internet and return it to its democratic roots.

It is a platform for building and deploying applications which do not need to rely on trust and cannot be controlled by any central authority.

    – Ethereum Foundation

The goal of Ethereum is to become the "blockchain of blockchains" or, more grandly, the "world computer." The Ethereum blockchain is a radically decentralized political and social order which is being built out of the millions of smart contracts that make up that blockchain.

Anyone may join Ethereum. And anyone who joins is free to upload all of his smart contracts, his digital information, and his computer programs to the Ethereum blockchain. While cryptocurrency blockchains are focused solely on cryptocurrencies, Ethereum is being constructed so that it will be able to run any program, or store any form of digital information, that can be embedded on a blockchain.

Currently, Ethereum's main problem is the slowness of its transaction speeds. Its transactions run slowly because it is necessary to constantly update every copy of the blockchain across a decentralized network of thousands of computers. And as Ethereum grows that transactional performance worsens. This is a major technical roadblock.

There are a number of major projects that are currently engaged in trying to find ways to speed up transaction times. Sharding is one strategy that randomly limits the number of computer nodes over which transactions have to be updated as a way of speeding up the network. By randomly limiting the number of nodes that process transactions, the blockchain as a whole does not have to be constantly updated. Only part of the blockchain is updated, while general updates occur much less often.

The Raiden Network is another project that attempts to deal with transaction speeds. Using this network, many or most Ethereum transactions will take place off the Ethereum blockchain. The Raiden Network guarantees a high degree of security for those off-blockchain transactions until the full blockchain is updated. Essentially, the Raiden Network allows people to "write checks" that can later be "cashed" by the full Ethereum blockchain. In early 2018, the Raiden Network was undergoing testing.

There are other solutions also in the works, including solutions created by blockchain rivals to Ethereum, such as Eos and Cardano.

As with all decentralized blockchains, no one owns or runs Ethereum. The Ethereum blockchain is guaranteed to run according to the rules that are permanently embedded in its code, rules that cannot easily be changed. This inability to easily change the code can, of course, cause problems. However, if a major crisis occurs and a change in the rules becomes absolutely necessary, it is possible to create what is called a "fork" in the blockchain. A fork occurs when a significant number of people on a blockchain decide to "port" the current blockchain to a new version of the chain. This creates two blockchains where there was only one before. And those people on the old blockchain must now decide whether they want to remain on the old version or to join the new blockchain.

In short, the political concept called "secession" is built into Ethereum by design. Not too surprisingly, a major fork of the Ethereum blockchain has already happened. There are today two major versions of Ethereum, one that is called "Ethereum Classic," which is the original version, and one called simply "Ethereum." Ethereum classic is the much smaller community.

The reason for the fork was that a major bug in the original blockchain had allowed hackers to steal many millions of Ether, the main Ethereum cryptocurrency. But since they committed this theft in accordance with the embedded rules of the blockchain, technically it was not a theft at all. And so nothing could be done about the theft, at least within the rules of the original blockchain. But since a great many people lost a lot of money, the decision was made by Ethereum's prime movers to "fork" the blockchain and to create a new Ethereum. Since the new Ethereum did not "recognize" that the original theft had occurred, the original theft did not occur – at least for those who had left the original Ethereum. As for the thieves who were left on the old Ethereum, the money that they had stolen now radically declined in value as Ethereum Classic became a minor player.

Ether is the cryptocurrency of Ethereum. However, since Ethereum is a radically decentralized community, any cryptocurrency can be used on the blockchain, so long as the parties to a transaction agree to use that cryptocurrency. Members of Ethereum are even free to create their own cryptocurrencies, if they like. The only problem, as we noted earlier, is to find someone who will accept your cryptocurrency as payment.

However, Ethereum is not primarily a platform for the creation of cryptocurrencies. It exists to create something called a "Dapp." A Dapp is a "Decentralized Application." This is any computer program that can run as decentralized code on the Ethereum blockchain. And a Dapp can be used to create something called a DAO or a "Decentralized Autonomous Organization." Briefly, a DAO is any business or organization that is made up of smart contracts. A DAO is an organization that is embedded as a series of smart contracts on the blockchain.

Anyone who creates a DAO will generally want to intervene in its ongoing operations. Also, most people will set up DAOs to generate profits for themselves. But a DAO could be set up as a non-profit organization. Or it could be set up distribute its profits to others.

In theory, a DAO could be created that is completely free of human control. Once this form of the DAO is set in motion, it would operate entirely according to the rules of the smart contracts that make it up, with no further human input.

For example, imagine a self-governing DAO that owns and operates a business. The DAO could be initially programmed to hire and fire its own employees according to defined criteria. It could be programmed to procure the necessary supplies for its business on a recurring basis and to create additional smart contracts as its business expands. It could hire its own lawyers if someone sues it.

All of this may seem a bit far-fetched, but a DAO could easily replace a company like Uber, which is little more than a software system that manages inputs between subcontracting drivers and customers. A DAO version of Uber would vet potential drivers and riders according to pre-established criteria and match them online. No human beings, other than the drivers and riders themselves, would be needed. And even the drivers could eventually be replaced by driverless cars.

Needless to say, the concept of a DAO would pose a challenge to our current legal system. The main legal problem is this: since a chain of smart contracts on a blockchain is almost unstoppable, laws will have to be reconfigured so as to be able to deal with such contracts. Laws will probably be needed to require that every smart contract that is embedded on a blockchain will have to be vetted first for its legality, because once a smart contract is on the blockchain it cannot be stopped, at least not without major complications.

How many people are currently on the Ethereum blockchain? It is impossible to get an exact number. However, in mid-January of 2018, there were more than 21 million unique addresses on the Ethereum network.[1] However, since individuals can own as many addresses as they want and since every smart contract has an address, the probable number of people on Ethereum is probably in the low millions. Still, in mid-January of 2018, there were over a million transactions per day on Ethereum.[2]

How many major organizations are involved with Ethereum? According to Wikipedia: "In March 2017, various blockchain start-ups, research groups, and Fortune 500 companies announced the creation of the Enterprise Ethereum Alliance (EEA) with 30 founding members… By July 2017, there were over 150 members in the Alliance." This included such major corporations as Toyota, Samsung, Microsoft, Intel, BNY Mellon, the National Bank of Canada, MasterCard, and Cisco Systems.

Here it is probably useful to stand back from Ethereum and look at the broader financial revolution that is going on, much of which is not yet on any blockchain. "Fintech," or software that is rapidly hollowing out the major financial institutions, is the driving force behind this revolution. Currently, new Fintech startups that are in direct competition with major financial institutions have an estimated collective value of 120 billion dollars.

However, there is an asymmetry in the current Fintech war between the new start-ups and older financial institutions. The major banks and insurance companies are using Fintech software to radically slim themselves down, while the Fintech startups tend to specialize in creating new kinds of financial services.

Banks make money by lending. It is the spread between the interest rates paid by the banks to their depositors and people to whom they lend money that constitutes the bank's profit. And those profits can be substantial. They are substantial enough that they allow the major banks and other financial institutions to employ tens of thousands of people and to own thousands of large buildings on prime real estate.

The new lending startups, however, are largely composed of automated software. They have very few employees and almost no real estate. And they generally engage in forms of lending that are largely free of government regulation. For one thing, they do not guarantee the safety of their depositors' money. But the profits both for them, and for their depositors, can be quite large.

For anyone who wants to obtain a loan at a regulated

bank, professionals at that bank will have to walk them through some complicated paperwork, while doing a detailed examination of their financial history. But online lenders present their customers with a simple online form that has only a few fields to be filled out. Nor are they interested in their customers' financial history, beyond employing a simple data set that will confirm their basic financial stability.

Because there are no government guarantees for depositors, the interest that can be paid to them is far higher than the interest paid to depositors in a traditional bank. Simultaneously, the interest that is charged to borrowers is much lower than that charged by the banks. Although online lenders will make less money overall at both ends of the process, they will have higher profits because they have radically streamlined the whole process. Unsurprisingly, the major banks are trying to imitate this success. They are engaged in radically downsizing their own work forces and eliminating their real estate holdings. This competitive war is reshaping the financial industry.

The new Fintech start-ups also threaten traditional insurance companies. Fintech start-ups now sell health, auto, and life insurance online. They are also engaged in creating new financial products that are not highly regulated by the government. In response, the major insurance companies are racing to downsize and streamline their own operations.

There is even a new kind of financial software called a "robo-advisor." This is an automated program that can replace most of what human financial advisors do. Interestingly, many of the start-ups in this field are working with the established banks and other institutions to help them create robo-advisors.

Some Fintech companies use blockchains, but most are not yet involved with them. However, at some point it is likely that most such businesses will be located on a blockchain.

Ethereum may or may not become the "blockchain of blockchains," but for the moment it is the main player in the blockchain world.

Notes:

1. etherscan.io/chart/address
2. etherscan.io/chart/tx

For more information go to: **www.ethereum.org**

The best book length introduction is *Ethereum: blockchains, digital assets, smart contracts, decentralized autonomous organizations* by Henning Diedrich (2016).

See also online videos by Vitalik Buterin, Ethereum's creator.

Hashgraph: Beyond the Blockchain

Although the hashgraph has been around for a few years as a private enterprise, I first learned of it before the first draft of this book was complete. Hashgraph claims to be a game changer. However, many of those working in the blockchain space remain skeptical.

With the announcement of a public version of the hashgraph in March 2018, called the Hedera hashgraph, it soon became clear that the hashgraph might very well be a giant leap beyond the blockchain. Some even compared the relationship between the blockchain and the hashgraph to the relationship between a propeller-driven aircraft and a supersonic jet.

In one sense, the hashgraph is simply another form of the blockchain, since it too is a distributed ledger. But in another sense, the hashgraph is not a blockchain at all, since it contains neither blocks nor chains. It contains hashes and graphs.

As we have already noted, any information that is embedded on a blockchain is guaranteed to be unalterable. This is because there are thousands of copies of a blockchain located on thousands of computers around the world. If some of those copies, or even many of them, are illicitly altered, those alterations can be easily discovered and the altered copies easily expelled from the network. That is how blockchains work.

However, this iron-clad guarantee of inalterability comes at a substantial cost in both energy consumption and in the slowness of transaction speeds. For the thousands of copies of a blockchain will become longer and longer over time as information is added to them. Also, the more transactions that occur on a blockchain the more often those thousands of copies have to be updated. The process of adding to the length of the blockchain and engaging in more and more transactions seriously begins to slow transaction speed, while consuming more and more energy to update the network. Thus if Bitcoin suddenly became a major world currency, Bitcoin transactions would literally need to consume all of the electricity currently being produced in the world, while Bitcoin transactions would take forever to complete.

These are major problems.

A number of promising software projects are underway that have the goals of radically reducing energy usage and of speeding up transaction times on the blockchain. But, at least so far, none of these projects has done more than mitigate the underlying problems.

The hashgraph solves those problems.

So what are hashes and graphs?

Like a blockchain network, a hashgraph network contains thousands of computer nodes that are in communication with each other. Like a blockchain network, a hashgraph node communicates the occurrence of a transaction to all the other nodes on the network. But unlike a blockchain network, the thousands of nodes on a hashgraph network do not continuously update thousands of copies of a blockchain. There are no copies to be updated. Instead, each node simply passes along the latest information, or "gossip," about a transaction to all the other nodes on the network, which adds that information incrementally to its database. A "gossip protocol," together with several other features, will ensure that the details of the transaction can never be altered.

Hashgraph is a very different system.

For example, suppose that one hashgraph node reports a transaction to the network. The node creates a cryptographic hash of the details of the transaction and time stamps that hash. The hash will also contain the identity of the node from which the hash is being sent as well as the identities of the nodes to which the hash is being sent. And the message is sent, not to every node on the network, but to a random choice of a few nodes. Those few nodes then add their own time-stamp and identities to the hash and randomly send the message on to a few other nodes.

This is repeated until all the nodes in the network have received the hash. Therefore the final hash will contain the complete history, and time stamps, and identities, of every node through which the hash has passed. It is this that creates the graph part of the hashgraph. It is possible to reconstruct a complete graph of that history of transmission.

Now from this bare description, it might appear to the reader that it would take a very long time for all the nodes on the network to receive the message of a particular transaction. But the actual process occurs in the blink of an eye. Leemon Baird, the mathematician who is largely responsible for creating the hashgraph, describes the process as follows: "if you have a million nodes talking to each other, in twenty syncs your message gets out to everybody. And if you're syncing twenty times a second, in one second your message gets out to everybody." The process is just that fast.

But it is the graph of the history of the hash's progress through the network that ensures that the information contained in the hash cannot be altered. Because every node time-stamps the hash as it passes it along, as well as adding its own identify to that hash, the graph that can be produced will show the complete history of that hash's communication across the network. Nor does this history have to be fully reconstructed to establish that the recorded transaction has not been altered. It is mathematically possible, through a "sampling" of that history, to prove that the record of the transmission of that transaction through the network is accurate.

Let us assume that someone tries to corrupt the process. Let us assume that a different hash, contradicting the information about the transaction, is also sent through the network and that some nodes used false time stamps. However, the transmission of this false hash is easily detected. Because each step in the corrupt message has also to be time-stamped by every node, it becomes easy to detect which nodes are adding the false time stamps.

Now one might think that creating a full historical record of how a message passes through thousands of nodes, with each node's time stamp and identity added as further hashes, might be as energy intensive and as slow to transact as updating all the copies of a blockchain network. But the addition of the time stamps and the nodal identities to a hash, which are cryptographically hashed and thus compressed, involves the addition of very little extra information. The energy needed to incrementally process all of these messages is quite small compared to the energy needed to update an entire blockchain and transaction speeds are nearly instantaneous.

Interestingly, some of the key computational elements that make up the hashgraph, for example the "gossip protocol," have long been known to computer scientists. But they have never been used in the combination that Leemon Baird has employed to create the hashgraph.

Swirlds, the company established by Baird and his colleague Mance Harmon, holds a series of patents on the hashgraph. Over the past several years, Swirlds has been engaged in creating private versions of the hashgraph for use by major corporations and has been very successful in finding major customers.

In March 2018, Swirlds unveiled a public version of the hashgraph, which they call Hedera. Hedera has been permanently licensed to a non-profit corporation which will oversee its public use. Everyone online will be allowed access to the Hedera hashgraph in order to create their own smart contracts and distributed organizations on the network, just as everyone is allowed to participate on the Ethereum blockchain. Indeed, smart contracts created on the Ethereum blockchain can be easily transferred to Hedera.

Hedera seems to be a blockchain killer.

Hedera transaction speeds are astonishing. Currently, the Bitcoin blockchain runs 10 transactions per second, while the Ethereum blockchain runs 25 transactions per second. Major credit card companies currently average 2,000 transactions per second and can reach peaks of 50,000 transactions per second. Hedera's world-wide test network easily cruises at 50,000 transactions per second and has the capability of engaging in hundreds of thousands of transactions per second.

Today, you can use Bitcoin to buy a cup of coffee. The problem is that very few coffee shops accept Bitcoin. This is because the transaction fees for Bitcoin purchases are many times the cost of the cup of coffee. And you will have to wait long enough for the transaction to complete that your coffee will certainly be cold. When Hedera is fully functional, on the other hand, you will be paying a transaction fee of a hundredth of a cent to buy a hot cup of coffee in real time.

One immediate expected use of Hedera is by multi-player, online games. Today, multi-player online games involve huge numbers of people. They thus require dedicated computer servers and networks, which involve large monthly fees. There are also latency problems in which players often have to wait while the game "catches up" with what they are doing. And this sets definite limits as to how complicated multi-player, online games can be. However, Hedera will enable millions of people to play much more complicated games online simultaneously with virtually no latency. Also, servers and dedicated networks will no longer be necessary, since each computer engaged in playing the game will be its own server. Playing fees will radically fall.

Hedera changes everything.

There is, however, one major problem. And that is Hedera's governance.

When we began our analysis of the new technologies, we examined a software project called Urbit. Although Urbit is not yet ready for public launch, and will probably not be ready for some time, those working on Urbit are in the process of creating a radically new Internet. They are engaged in creating a radical decentralization of the operating systems of both the

Internet and of the personal computer, which will be merged into a single software system. Urbit will be a peer-to-peer, completely decentralized system. No third party platforms will be needed in the Urbit universe. If successful, Urbit will be a game-changer. It will radically decentralize computing and the Internet, destroying the Big Tech platforms.

The reader may recall that the projected governance of Urbit is that of a "digital republic." Although a minority within the Urbit universe will control the underlying Urbit code, this control will be limited. The Urbit network will be a hierarchy of three classes of users: "galaxies," "stars," and "planets." Code changes will be made as the result of a consensus among those who own the galaxy and star properties, while most Urbit users will own planet properties. However, anyone who dissents from a change in the code will have the ability to secede from those who adopt the change. If a star disagrees with the galaxy to which it is attached, the star is free to leave and attach itself to a different galaxy. And if a planet disagrees with the star to which it is attached, the planet can leave for a different star.

Urbit is a federated republic.

The governance of the Ethereum blockchain is also radically decentralized. Ethereum governance is essentially the sum of individual smart contracts that make up the Ethereum blockchain. However, as in Urbit, the overall control of the Ethereum code, and of changes made to that code, will be in the hands of a relatively small number of people. But they must convince most of those who participate in the Ethereum network to adopt any changes that they propose. If a major public disagreement occurs, as happened early in Ethereum's existence, the blockchain will then be "forked." In other words, it will be broken up into two independent blockchains, with each blockchain going its own way.

The Hedera hashgraph is as radically decentralized in its operations as Urbit and Ethereum. There is no governing authority in the daily operations of the network. But the decision has been made by the patent owners that there will be a governing body of the public version of the hashgraph – there will be only one public version allowed – and that this governing body will be a centralized organization. The governing body will be made up of a board of representatives from 39 elite corporations and other major institutions from around the world. The institutions that serve on the board will rotate over time, while a central committee made up of a few members of the board will make the decisions as to which corporations will next serve on the board. It is the serving corporations who will elect the members of this central committee. Let us call this central committee "the Supreme Soviet."

With Hedera, the problem of the centralization of power definitely returns. A rotating, global oligarchy will control the Hedera hashgraph.

Now the owners of the Hedera hashgraph have promised that everyone in the world will be welcome to participate on the network and that everyone will have complete freedom to create smart contracts and to interact with each other on Hedera. However, as anyone with a rudimentary knowledge of centralized systems knows, such promises mean very little. All that matters is who actually governs. Since it will be progressive-converged international corporations and other institutions that will control Hedera, it is almost certain that this promise of freedom will be violated, if anyone on the Hedera hashgraph does not conform to the progressive understanding of reality.

This is why the creation of the Hedera hashgraph is a major strategic disaster for anti-progressives.

There are two possible responses to this situation.

The first is for anti-progressives to have nothing at all to do with the Hedera hashgraph. Currently, a number of projects are underway that have the goal of greatly speeding up the blockchain and of radically cutting energy usage. Some of these projects promise great success, even if that promised success is a year or more away. Of course, the existence of Hedera may inspire projects that might find a way to bypass the Hedera advantage. There is also Urbit in the wings, which will be as fast as Hedera. However, since Urbit is neither a blockchain nor a hashgraph, it will not be able to provide a "trustless" guarantee of immutably held information. It will, however, provide a guarantee of freedom.

The second is to join the Hedera platform and to fight the progressive corporations who control it by trying to shame them into keeping their promise of a free public arena. In the long run, this strategy will not work. Progressive arrogance, the progressive lust to virtuously rule over others, and the increasingly hallucinatory nature of progressive beliefs, will ensure that at some point the Hedera hashgraph will become toxic.

Still: the rise of Hedera marks the beginning of the end of the Big Tech platforms.

Notes:

"A Simple Explanation of Hashgraph with Pictures"
https://www.youtube.com/watch?v=wgwYU1Zr9Tg

For a general, although somewhat technical, overview of hashgraph, which occurred before the public announcement of Hedera, watch the Harvard lecture by Leemon Baird at:
https://www.youtube.com/watch?v=p0c231Jw71s.

For an overview of Hedera's oligarchical governance:
www.hederahashgraph.com/council

Although this document straightforwardly describes a centralized governance for Hedera, the magic word "decentralized" is sprinkled throughout as if that word actually described Hedera's governance.

Summary and Conclusion

This book began with the observation that progressive beliefs are little more than a rationalization for the centralization of power. Although those beliefs seem to be about questions of human equality, it is the desire to control every aspect of society that motivates the progressive elite.

If American society were once more suddenly and irrevocably decentralized in its actual operations, progressive beliefs would evaporate into thin air. This is because those beliefs have no reason to exist except as a rationalization of centralized power. Other forms of evil, of course, would arise to take the place of progressivism. We live, after all, in a fallen world. But the particular evil called progressivism would cease to exist.

The technological revolution of our era, resting upon the creation of the personal computer and the Internet, began as a system of peer-to-peer communications that promised a radically decentralized future. During the nineties, there were many who believed, with good reason, that this technological revolution would abolish most centralized authorities.

Instead, a hyper-centralization of social authority occurred. During the first two decades of the twenty-first century, what became Big Tech created huge, centralized platforms online that came to control the online experience of most Americans. Big Tech also created the tools that permitted them to engage in an unceasing surveillance of everyone who was online. Big Tech seemed to be on the verge of creating a hyper-centralized political and social order, while hovering in the background were the security organs of the national state.

Yet it is still possible to argue that the technological revolution is leading us to a radically decentralized future. For the next steps in that revolution, as we have detailed in this essay, are all forms of radical decentralization. Even the Hedera hashgraph, with its projected centralized governance, is an attempt to centrally govern a system that is inherently decentralized.

We began this study with an analysis of Urbit, a project to create a new kind of Internet, based upon the radical decentralization of the software that will control both the Internet and the personal computer.

We then went on to analyze various aspects of what is called the "Blockchain Revolution." Those strategies include smart contracts, cryptocurrencies, and block-chain communities like Ethereum. In all these areas, software solutions are being created that are far more sophisticated versions of the peer-to-peer network of the nineties.

Even Fintech, today's corporate technology, is part of this rising revolution of decentralized software. The major banks and financial corporations are employing Fintech to radically decentralize their operations, with the ultimate prospect of the self-abolition of the financial corporation.

But it is the overall direction of the revolution in technology that points to the radical decentralization of all our interactions online and thus also points to the coming destruction of progressivism.

While it is necessary to fight the current battles against Big Tech's attempt to purge anti-progressives from the Internet, the real battle for the future lies in the creation of software systems that will radically decentralize society. And the faster the pace of this decentralization, the more likely it will be that progressivism can be destroyed before it destroys America.

Made in the USA
Coppell, TX
07 April 2021